D0867718

# PROFESSORS AS TEACHERS

# Professors as Teachers

Steven M. Cahn

RESOURCE *Publications* · Eugene, Oregon

PROFESSORS AS TEACHERS

Resource Publications
An Imprint of Wipf and Stock Publishers
199 W. 8th Ave., Suite 3
Eugene, OR 97401

www.wipfandstock.com

PAPERBACK ISBN: 978-1-6667-4637-2
HARDCOVER ISBN: 978-1-6667-4638-9
EBOOK ISBN: 978-1-6667-4639-6

JUNE 29, 2022 9:10 AM

# Contents

# PREFACE

THE TITLE OF THIS BOOK is ironic, for too many professors view themselves primarily not as teachers but researchers. Indeed, their lack of concern for pedagogic responsibilities may burden colleagues and harm students. I recognize, of course, that some faculty members give teaching their all. The problem, however, is that by every account these instructors are the minority.

How can the system be changed so that success in the classroom will be promoted and receive greater emphasis? Presenting proposals to achieve that end is my focus. I have drawn freely on my previous writings but have reworked them to offer a unified presentation.

Here are my sources:

Cahn, Steven M., *The Eclipse of Excellence: A Critique of American Higher Education*. Public Affairs Press, 1973. Reprinted by Wipf and Stock Publishers, 2004.

———, *Education and the Democratic Ideal*. Nelson Hall Company, 1979. Reprinted by Wipf and Stock Publishers, 2004.

———, *Saints and Scamps: Ethics in Academia*. Rowman & Littlefield, 1986. Revised Edition, 1994. 25th Anniversary Edition, 2011.

———, *Puzzles & Perplexities: Collected Essays*. Rowman & Littlefield, 2002. Second Edition, 2007.

———, *From Student to Scholar: A Candid Guide to Becoming a Professor*. Columbia University Press, 2008.

————, *Teaching Philosophy: A Guide*. Routledge, 2018.

————, *Inside Academia: Professors, Politics, and Policies*. Rutgers University Press, 2019.

————, *Navigating Academic Life: How the System Works*. Routledge, 2021.

I am indebted to Mary Ann McHugh of Arizona State University for many stylistic suggestions. I also thank the staff at Wipf and Stock Publishers for their support; working again with them has been a pleasure. As always, I am grateful to my brother, Victor L. Cahn, for his advice on matters literary and otherwise, and to my wife, Marilyn Ross, M.D., for more than I can express in words.

## Chapter 1

# TEACHING AND RESEARCH

WHEN ELEMENTARY AND SECONDARY school teachers are asked what they do for a living, they typically answer, "I'm a teacher." The usual follow-up, "What do you teach?" elicits replies such as "Second Grade," or "Middle School," or "English and History," or "French and Latin." When, on the other hand, college professors are asked what they do, they usually identify as physicists, economists, literary critics, and so on. Their primary commitment is to their discipline, not their classes.

The typical professorial goal, professional advancement, is pursued by publishing in scholarly journals, authoring or editing books with university presses and similar publishers, participating in academic conferences, and presenting lectures at colleges or universities. Such activities help build a strong academic reputation, leading to more prestigious invitations, appointments, and honors.

In no way does teaching promote one's academic career. For that reason, many view time spent in the classroom not as a positive feature of the profession but as a drawback.

Typical was a comment I overheard years ago at a meeting of the American Philosophical Association. A group of graduate students was responding enthusiastically as one described a position for which he had just been interviewed. "It's a great job," he told his friends. "There's very little teaching, and I'll have plenty of time for my work." What he failed to recognize is that teaching *was* his work.

During the years I served as an administrator, one of my major responsibilities was interviewing candidates for faculty positions. When I inquired about requests they might have, invariably they asked for the fewest possible number of courses to teach. Those professors who were teaching three courses per semester at their school hoped to be given two; those who already taught two sought to do one; those with one per semester looked for one per year. Some even expressed a desire to begin their association by being awarded a year's sabbatical, thus allowing them time to complete a current research project. My award for audacity goes to the applicant who wondered if he might start with a two-year sabbatical.

Indeed, in academic jargon instructional hours are known as a "load." Research, however, is referred to as an "opportunity." Faculty members would think any colleague daft who announced: "Good news. My research load has been reduced, and I'll have more opportunity to teach."

The emphasis on pursuing research but minimizing teaching was apparent during the many years I was a member of the Philosophy Program at the City University of New York (CUNY) Graduate Center. Each September my colleagues offered an orientation session for new doctoral students. Often the first question posed to them was What's your specialty? Those who replied with uncertainty received patronizing smiles, while the response "I plan to teach" invariably caused derisive laughter.

In all candor, that answer would have been the one I myself would have offered. I wanted to be a teacher, preferably but not necessarily at the college level. As an undergraduate I had found more success in my philosophy classes than in my other areas of interest, including mathematics, history, political science, and musicology. Hence I chose to enter graduate school in philosophy.

Regarding my planned specialty, I didn't have one. As matters turned out, the areas in which I later published were primarily interests I developed after having earned my doctorate.

Decades later, when two of my former students, Professors Robert B. Talisse and Maureen Eckert, expressed an interest in presenting me with a Festschrift, they asked me for an appropriate title for the book. I replied almost immediately, "A Teacher's Life." To this day, when I am asked what I did for a living, I answer, "I was a teacher." I may not be asked any subsequent questions as to what, where, or whom I taught, but I take pleasure in identifying students as the primary focus of my life's work.

Admittedly, my degree of success in the classroom does not match that achieved by some others. I take second place to no one, however, in my admiration for the performance of those I consider great teachers. Yet to other members in the department of a celebrated teacher, the situation can be perturbing. Few are comfortable admitting that their colleague's class size is largely due to that individual's superior teaching skills. In such a situation, the inclination is to chalk up their colleague's success to mere personal popularity. Indeed, in an effort to prevent too many students from registering for a course with an acclaimed instructor, a department may place an arbitrary limit on class size and thereby hope to maintain the absurd fiction that all its members are equally skilled in the classroom.

Administrators, too, strongly favor the renowned researcher over the best of instructors. After all, having on the faculty a national or international authority brings prestige to the entire institution and in the sciences as well as the social sciences attracts outside funding that contributes significantly to the school's coffers. The superb instructor, though, is only a local celebrity, legendary perhaps on campus but unknown outside its gates. For those reasons, leading researchers have leverage with the administration in a way leading teachers do not.

In sum, while almost all administrators claim to value teaching, their actions tell otherwise. When evaluating a candidate for a faculty position, they typically favor the most promising researcher. When a faculty member is considered for tenure, a top-notch scholar who is barely adequate as a teacher is far more likely to be approved than a superb instructor whose scholarly record is thin. And when another institution recruits a faculty member, little effort is made to retain those who have focussed primarily on achieving excellence in the classroom.

Granted, a school may give teaching prizes to a select few while rewarding research for the many, but such an initiative does not fool anyone on campus about the administration's priorities. After all, what is virtually unheard of is giving research prizes to a select few while rewarding teaching for the many. In short, research rules in academia, as everyone there knows.

Students may enter college assuming that, as in elementary or high school, they are the center of attention. Soon enough, however, they learn otherwise. Although students pay tuition, the faculty's focus is elsewhere.

Can anything be done to change the present system? I believe so, and in what follows I offer five substantive suggestions.

*Chapter 2*

# How Teachers Succeed

Before proceeding to present proposals, though, I want to describe the elements of effective teaching. They were embodied for me by a few inspired and inspiring faculty members with whom I studied at Columbia. As an undergraduate in the College, I was strongly influenced by Montaigne scholar Donald Frame; translator of Spanish and Portuguese Gregory Rabassa; charismatic American historian James P. Shenton; intellectual historian Bernard W. Wishy; distinguished musicologist William J. Mitchell; conductor of the Goldman Band and expert on contemporary music Richard Franko Goldman; and eminent philosopher of science Ernest Nagel, who encouraged me to pursue the study of philosophy. Then in Columbia's Graduate School of Arts and Sciences, I had the pleasure of studying with the eloquent political philosopher Charles Frankel, who subsequently became U.S. Assistant Secretary of State for Educational and Cultural Affairs, then president and director of the National Humanities Center. Most significantly for me, my dissertation advisor was the prominent metaphysician Richard Taylor, whose impact on my career was immense, as he guided me step by step through the thickets of academia. None of these teachers is still living, but their influence on me remains strong.

They all had remarkably different styles, but each excelled in the art of leading students to master a subject while arousing appreciation for it. Such in essence is the teacher's goal, far easier to describe than to achieve.

To illustrate the problem, imagine trying to explain baseball to a person unfamiliar with the sport. Where would you begin? With the roles of the pitcher and catcher? How about the calling of balls and strikes? Or the location of the bases, how to score runs, or the ways outs can be made? The fundamental difficulty is that all these starting points presume knowledge of some of the others. How, then, can you break the circle of intertwining concepts and render the subject both accessible and appealing?

Next consider teaching a course in calculus, Chinese, or the history of Africa. Any of these subjects is far more complex than baseball. Moreover, rather than a single listener, a class contains many students with varying skills, interests, and backgrounds. Thus reaching the entire group is daunting.

To be blunt, teaching is hard. Only those who have never tried might think otherwise. Indeed, even with a thorough understanding of a subject, conveying that knowledge can be frustrating for all involved. Yet some instructors, like those I mentioned, succeed to an amazing degree.

Now the crucial question: What do those teachers have in common that others lack?

The answer is *not* that successful teachers invariably know the subject better than others. Rather, they have mastered pedagogical skills that, surprising to some, are the same whether the students are children, teenagers, or adults.

Show me a terrific fifth-grade teacher, and I'll show you someone who with specialist study could become an outstanding instructor at the collegiate level. Show me a boring college professor, and I'll show you someone who would be equally tiresome to a class of ten-year-olds.

One difference, however, is that ten-year-olds faced with ineffective teaching are likely to react by yelling or throwing things; poorly taught college students simply open their phones.

But what are the fundamentals of pedagogic success? The essence is found in three strategic steps.

The first is commonly referred to as "motivation." Without it, a class stagnates. After all, how long will you watch a movie that does nothing to capture your attention? Or read a novel that begins with a situation of no interest? The slower the start, the more difficult to generate enthusiasm. At best, the audience allows you a few minutes without much action. The same with teaching.

Consider the openings of the following two lectures, delivered in the years 1969 and 1970 as the Presidential Addresses of the Eastern Division Meeting of the American Philosophical Association. Each was presented to an audience consisting of approximately five hundred philosophers.

In 1970 the speaker was the eminent American philosopher Wilfrid Sellars, who taught at the University of Pittsburgh. He began as follows: "The quotation which I have taken as my text occurs in the opening paragraphs of the Paralogisms of Pure Reason in which Kant undertakes a critique of what he calls 'Rational Psychology.' The paragraphs are common to the two editions of the *Critique of Pure Reason,* and the formulations they contain may be presumed to have continued to satisfy him—at least as introductory remarks."[1] If your interest in reading further is minimal, many in the audience shared that attitude, for although the subject matter was relevant to Kant scholars, not one word Sellars offered motivated his other listeners. What could he have done instead?

One answer is found in the address given a year earlier by the renowned British philosopher Stuart Hampshire, then teaching at Princeton University. He, too, wished to give an exposition of a text but offered a far more provocative opening: "I want to speak today about a philosophy of mind to which I will not at first assign an identity or date, except that its author could not have lived and worked before 1600. He is modern, in the sense that he thinks principally about the future applications of the physical sciences to the study of personality. As I speak, I hope that it will not at first be too easy for you to tell whether or not he is our contemporary, whether indeed he is not present in this room. I attempt this

---

1. *Proceedings and Addresses of The American Philosophical Association,* vol. XLIV (September, 1971), 5.

reconstruction as a way of praising a philosopher who has not, I think, been at all justly interpreted so far."[2]

Hampshire's withholding the name of the author was a brilliant stroke, because members of the audience were immediately curious as to whom he was referring. As they looked around, wondering if the subject was there, they also listened carefully, treating Hampshire's every sentence as a clue. Finally, a few minutes from his conclusion, Hampshire revealed that the author in question was Baruch Spinoza (1632–1677), and ended by quoting the passage from Spinoza's *Ethics* that had been the unspoken focus.

Had Hampshire begun by quoting the text he intended to discuss, the philosophical substance would have been unchanged, but doing so would have been a pedagogical misstep, for few would have listened with special care. But by making his talk a puzzle, Hampshire captivated his audience, and, having been present myself, I can testify that the rapt quiet in the hall was striking.

Hampshire's talk was no richer philosophically than that of Sellars. Pedagogically speaking, though, their two lectures were of vastly different quality.

Here's another example of effective motivation, coming not from the acme of the scholarly world but from a far more ordinary setting. The description is offered by my brother, Victor L. Cahn, now Professor Emeritus of English at Skidmore College. There he was a standout in the classroom, but his skills had been honed earlier in preparatory schools, including Pomfret School in Connecticut and Phillips Exeter Academy in New Hampshire. His first experience in that milieu took place at Mercersburg Academy in Pennsylvania. When he arrived as a novice, he observed a veteran instructor teaching a class in vocabulary study. No one, instructor or students, was engrossed by the activity.

The next day my brother was asked to take over the group. At first he began calling on the boys, much as his colleague had done, asking them to define words. He soon realized, however, that the students were bored, and so was he.

2. *Proceedings and Addresses of The American Philosophical Association*, vol. XLIII (September, 1970), 5.

Here in his own words is what happened.

After a timid answer from one student, [I] challenged the next: "Do you agree with that definition?"

"Yes."

"Are you sure?"

"I think so."

My eyebrows rose in feigned disbelief. "But I sense doubt. And our only way of resolving the uncertainty is to solicit another opinion."

As I began to fire questions around the room, the company before me sat up straight and began to grin. Gradually I became more animated, almost like a vaudevillian comic peppering the audience with one-liners. I heard myself call for words to be used in sentences, for two words to be used in the same sentence, for students to quiz one another, and for ever more complicated routines and games.

In the meantime I maintained a cheerful patter. "Bravo! And if I claimed to be 'abstemious,' would I be more or less rigorous in my self-denial than if I was 'ascetic'?"

And to the next: "Jack, would you consider that definition 'apt' or unnecessarily 'abstruse'? And, if so, why? And, if not, why not?"

And later,

"Bob, I see that we're nearing the end of this portion of the entertainment. I presume that leaves you feeling acrimonious."

"No, sir," with a smile.

"What do you mean, 'No, sir'? Are you implying that I have mischaracterized your mood?"

"I don't know, but you're using the wrong word," with a snicker.

My face registered shock. "Am I to understand that you have the temerity to correct my usage?"

"That's what I'm doing."

By now everyone was chuckling. "Allen, I see you find all this amusing. Then you must agree with Bob."

"He nailed you, sir!"

"But 'acrimonious' means 'pleased,' doesn't it?"

"Not even close. It means 'bitter.'"

"Scott, he's correcting me! Can you believe that?"

"Yes, sir."

"And can you think of a word that would describe his boldness in doing so?"

"How about 'audacious'?"

I continued in this manner for nearly half an hour, until everyone in the room was breathless.[3]

My brother's account profits from his being a playwright with numerous off-Broadway productions to his credit. His strategy in that classroom, though, offers several important pedagogic insights.

First, he was conscious of the tedium caused by his initial presentation. Too many unsuccessful teachers are unaware or uncaring of their impact on students. These instructors often ascribe a boring class to the students rather than the pedagogy.

On the contrary, when my brother recognized the situation, he picked up the pace, injected humor, and turned the class into a sort of show. By involving the students in the learning process and having them use key words in sentences rather than in isolation, he deepened their understanding while enhancing their enthusiasm.

In this case the motivational device was the style in which the material was presented as well as the personality of the instructor. That my brother has an endearing sense of humor surely benefits his teaching, but laughter in the classroom needs to be put in the service of learning, not treated as an end in itself. Yet if the instructor has a winning personality and can rely on it to interest students in the subject, so much the better.

I hasten to add, however, that successful teaching in a classroom doesn't require a lively demeanor outside it. In this regard I recall my experience at the Colby College Summer School of Languages, begun in 1948 with Swarthmore College but in 1955 becoming exclusively a Colby program, highly regarded until disbanded for financial reasons in 1968. Four languages were offered:

3. Victor L. Cahn, *Classroom Virtuoso: Reflections of a Life in Learning* (Lanham, MD: Rowman & Littlefield, 2009), 5–6.

French, German, Russian, and Spanish, each at the introductory, intermediate, and advanced levels. Outstanding instructors from various colleges participated, and I may have established a record by attending three times to study three different languages: Russian to meet a college language requirement, then French and German for my doctorate.

At the end of my stint with French, I told friends who had been studying German there that I planned to return the next summer to take on that language myself. Immediately they urged me to enroll in the section of grammar taught by Philip Bither, a graduate of Colby who had served on its faculty throughout his career. Having seen him on campus, I was perplexed by the recommendation. Professor Bither was a quiet man, who sought and attracted little attention. Why would I want to face a dull fellow teaching a dull subject?

Nevertheless, when the next summer arrived, I requested that he admit me to his section. He casually signed the necessary paper, but I remained apprehensive.

In the building where we met, bells indicated the beginning and end of classes; hence on the first day I sat with a dozen other students awaiting the instructor and the signal. Soon Professor Bither appeared, inexpressive as always.

Then the bell rang.

At once Professor Bither became a whirlwind, speaking quickly and decisively. As he rapidly went from student to student posing questions from our textbook, he compelled us to reply at his speed, not our own. If a student answered correctly, Professor Bither surprised us again. He did not move to the next student, a familiar pattern that encourages not listening to answers but looking ahead to figure out which question you will be asked. Instead he responded to the student who had answered correctly, "Good, take the next one." Then, after another correct answer, "Good, take another." The pace was frenetic. Finally when everyone was exhausted, the bell rang, and Professor Bither resumed his quiet demeanor and ambled out.

In sum, the course was unforgettable. I enjoyed learning German grammar but never again supposed I could predict how a teacher I had met outside of a classroom would perform within it.

I should add that many years later, while teaching at the University of Vermont (UVM), I was waiting for a bus one wintry day when a member of the German department joined me. Seeking a topic I thought might enliven the bleakness of the afternoon, I mentioned that one summer I had studied German at Colby College with Professor Philip Bither and inquired whether my colleague knew him. As it turned out he did, but expressed consolation at what he presumed had been my boredom. As the bus arrived and I was boarding, I looked back and said that on the contrary Professor Bither's classes were among the most exciting I had ever experienced. My colleague's face expressed sheer incredulity, as he wondered how the Philip Bither he knew could have taught an interesting course, or how I could have had such a strange reaction.

In Professor Bither's case, his style was the motivation. Few, however, can adopt such a passionate approach, but even any attempt to arouse interest will likely attract at least some students to follow where the teacher leads.

Yet even with a motivated student, a successful teacher needs to know how to take advantage of such interest. A second key element is organization, presenting material in a sequence that promotes understanding.

Teachers should try to ensure that each of their remarks will be understood by those with no prior knowledge of the subject. If an explanation leaves students baffled, the fault is not theirs but the teacher's. That principle may seem harsh, but, to repeat, effective teaching is daunting.

Recall the example of teaching baseball. Consider the following effort: "In playing baseball you try to score runs. Only the team to whom the ball is pitched can score. You run around the bases and try to avoid outs. Three strikes and you're out. The game has nine innings." This attempt at teaching is a failure. Not that any of the statements is false. Each is true yet not only disconnected from the previous ones but also presuming knowledge the listener doesn't possess.

The first statement refers to "runs," but the learner hasn't been told how a run is scored. The second statement refers to a ball being "pitched," but the role of the pitcher hasn't been explained. The remaining statements refer to "bases," "strikes," "outs," and "innings," but none of these terms has been put in context. In short, if you don't understand baseball, you won't learn much from these remarks. Thus an explanation can be factual yet pedagogically unsuccessful due to a lack of effective organization. (Incidentally, one strategy my brother suggested is to begin by presenting the diagram of a baseball field, indicating fair and foul territory, where the bases are located, the batter's potential route around them, and the placement of the pitcher, catcher, and fielders; with that information in hand, the concepts of outs, runs, balls and strikes, and innings will be comprehensible.)

Explaining fundamentals to the uninitiated requires patience. Poor teachers easily become upset as students find difficulty in following a subject's ins and outs. Yet instructors who gripe about the ineptitude of their students are akin to surgeons who complain that their patients are sick. Whether in the classroom or the operating room, problems should provide an intriguing challenge rather than a reason to become exasperated with those having difficulties.

Even a well-organized presentation, however, will not succeed without a third key element: clarity.

One problem is speaking too quickly. Whatever your content, if you speak too rapidly you won't be understood. Indeed, the most obvious sign of a poor lecturer is rushing. When those who are inexperienced come to a podium, they hardly ever speak at a proper pace. Yet when you hear a genuine orator, the sentences come slowly. No student will ever object to a teacher's speaking too deliberately, but many will complain if the words cascade.

Another cause of obscurity is using terms the audience doesn't understand. If I remark that for a year I worked at the NEH, which has a different mission from the NEA and is unconnected to the DOJ, Washington insiders will know that I'm referring to the

National Endowment for the Humanities, the National Endowment for the Arts, and the Department of Justice, but other listeners will be lost. Should they know these acronyms? Maybe, maybe not. Either way, if many are unfamiliar with them, that's reason enough not to use them without explanation.

Imagine listening to an instructor in an introductory course who says, "To paraphrase the author of the *Pastorals*, a sparse supply of cognition is a minatory entity." Few in any class are likely to understand this remark. If the problem is pointed out to the speaker, the irritated reply may be, "It's obvious I'm referring to Alexander Pope." "But who," a student might ask, "is Alexander Pope?" At this point the instructor is likely to burst out with frustration: "How can you not know?" Perhaps needless to say, this person is not cut out to be a teacher. And even if the students were told that Pope was a celebrated eighteenth-century English poet, they probably still wouldn't realize that the teacher was paraphrasing Pope's line "A little learning is a dangerous thing," which, in fact, may itself be unknown to many. And why use the word "minatory"? Hardly anyone will be familiar with its meaning, which is derived from the Latin word *minari*, meaning "to threaten." Yet inept teachers proceed in such confusing ways all the time.

Another reason for lack of clarity is omitting steps in reasoning. Suppose an instructor of first-year students who need to brush up on algebra says, "Given that $17-11 = 3x$, we know that $2x = 4$." Many students in the class won't understand. The teacher has failed to take the time to explain how the first equation proves that $x = 2$, thus $2 \times 2 = 4$.

The teacher might respond that the point is obvious. Well, it may be obvious to the teacher but not to all the students, and their comprehension should be the teacher's focus.

But can't you omit what seems apparent? The question brings to mind an incident, reported by a number of witnesses, involving Willard Van Orman Quine, one of the greatest logicians of the twentieth century and a professor of philosophy at Harvard University. His textbook on symbolic logic was widely used, and although he didn't relish teaching the subject, he was occasionally asked to do so. Once in such a course, after he wrote a proof on the board, a student raised his hand and asked impatiently, "Why bother writing out that proof? It's obvious." To which Quine replied, "Young man, this entire course is obvious."

In an introductory class everything taught may be obvious—obvious to the teacher but not to the students. The same may sometimes be true even in a graduate seminar.

A former colleague of mine at New York University (NYU), Kai Nielsen, was highly regarded as an undergraduate and graduate teacher. When asked the key to his success at any level, he replied, "Every course I teach is an introductory course." He meant that no matter how advanced the students were supposed to be, he never proceeded without explaining every step in his reasoning, so no one would become lost. Other notable professors who taught similarly were Rogers Albritton (philosophy) at Harvard University, Roderick Chisholm (philosophy) at Brown University, Rita Cooley (politics) at NYU, and Lillian Feder (English and comparative literature) at Queens College and the CUNY Graduate Center. I heard them all lecture, and their clarity was memorable. They weren't in the classroom to flaunt their erudition or display their brilliance; they were there to teach.

To sum up, when you find an instructor who motivates the class, organizes the material, and presents it clearly, you've found a successful teacher. And whether the audience are fifth graders, high school juniors, undergraduates, or PhD candidates, the same principles of effective teaching apply.

*Chapter 3*

# LEARNING TO TEACH

NOW FOR THE CENTRAL question: How can academic culture be changed to promote and highlight effective teaching? Graduate school is where individuals become oriented to professorial life. Thus that educational setting is the appropriate place to begin.

My first suggestion is that all graduate students seeking to be recommended for a faculty position should complete a departmental practicum that guides them in providing quality instruction to undergraduates. For many years I offered such a credit-bearing course in the Philosophy Program at the CUNY Graduate Center, and the results were dramatic.

While some class time was spent exploring ethical obligations and pedagogic principles, as well as strategies for testing and grading (two subjects I shall discuss subsequently), most of the hours were devoted to practice. Each of the approximately fifteen students gave a series of five-to-ten-minute presentations intended for an introductory class, after which the speaker received immediate feedback, first from the other students, then from me. If, during the talk, someone did not understand the speaker, that listener was asked to raise a hand without delay, thereby requesting further explanation.

At first, most of the participants were nervous as they stood before the audience. They mumbled, talked too fast, relied on oral tics such as "y'know," "right," or "OK," laughed self-consciously, and stared at the ceiling, the chalkboard, or their notes, avoiding eye contact with those they were supposed to be addressing. They made little attempt to interest their listeners in the subject and offered few, if any, clarifying examples. They asked questions without giving any student the opportunity to answer. They used technical terms without explaining them and introduced ideas without proper foundation, thus provoking numerous raised hands. In general, the speakers lacked energy. In short, these beginners displayed all the pedagogical shortcomings that turn too many classrooms into scenes of confusion and apathy.

But whereas most instructors who communicate inadequately are never called to account, in our practicum weak presentations immediately elicited a series of constructive suggestions. Not only did these help each individual, but they reinforced for all participants the elements of effective instruction.

These efforts soon yielded noticeable improvements. The students began to speak more slowly, motivate their audience, organize and clarify their presentations, and avoid the most common classroom pitfalls.

Lecturers exhibited greater energy, and some whose initial stage fright had made them seem somber or remote turned out, after becoming more at ease, to be engaging and even humorous.

Those who displayed marked improvement received generous plaudits from the others, and the developing esprit de corps encouraged all to try to enhance their performance. Before long, the talks became quite compelling, and even the few students who continued to struggle were conscious of the steps needed to improve.

After listening to each of the final presentations, all the participants wrote reactions that I later shared anonymously at a personal conference with each member of the class. Perhaps I can convey most effectively what we accomplished by quoting a sampling of these comments, each condensed but using the exact words of a respondent. (I am especially grateful to Jordan Pascoe, now a professor of philosophy at Manhattan College, for many of these perceptive observations.)

- Energetic, attention-grabbing, and polished presentation. Nice motivation, leading expertly to the topic to be discussed. Smooth interaction with students; handled comments well without distraction. Clear exposition of the issues at hand. Should avoid using notes too much. Should slow down a bit.

- Way too many "OKs." Too much looking at the board. No attempt at motivation. Many opportunities for discussion passed over. Though he asked us to raise our hands if we had a comment, there didn't seem to be any opportunities to do so.

- Powerful example used to motivate interest. The pace at times was a bit fast, perhaps because of nervousness. You asked questions but mostly answered them yourself. I think this made for a certain disengagement on the part of the class. It's hard to hold interest by just talking to the class. You need to connect to them.

- Became much more comfortable toward the end, warmed up, relaxed. You became able to use emphasis and tone to create drama, suspense, and interest. Nice, personable manner, and slow, clear pace.

- Don't look at the board like you're expecting it to do something. Make sure you're making eye contact with us. Your tone is calm and reassuring. Great use of example to build the point. You use the class and their answers well. It becomes a fun discussion.

- The pacing was a little fast in some places. Examples worked well, but I think that discussing them further, especially by asking students to participate at some point, would have worked even better. Overall, a lively and interesting presentation of a difficult topic.

- There's no motivation, no gateway into the issue. Way too attached to notes. Put them down. We desperately need examples. There's too much terminology tossed about, and nothing relevant or playful to tie it down. The main thrust of your attention is the board. Make the students your primary focus.

- Considerably more comfortable and casual than in previous presentations. Good use of humor to engage audience. Much better job of making eye contact and connecting with the class. A lot of information is covered a little too quickly. It would be a good idea to use the board to set up and outline and keep track of key terms. But overall so much better. Congratulations!

Over the years I learned that students who excelled at teaching were likely to have had a background in some variety of public performance. Among the standouts were a former ballet dancer, a trumpeter, and a magician, all of whom had learned how to keep the attention of an audience.

But even many of those who lacked such an advantage made major strides. One who began timorously told me later that when at his school peer evaluators observed his teaching, he received high praise for the slow pace at which he spoke and the clarity of his explanations. In another case, a student who struggled throughout the course informed me years later that he had continued to work on lessons he had learned in the practicum and was proud to say that at the college where he now taught he had just been awarded a prize for excellence in teaching.

Note that while talking about teaching has its place, a crucial step to improvement is practice followed by constructive criticism. No one has ever become a pianist, tennis player, or bicyclist just by listening to lectures or participating in discussions. Performance is required, as it is for the enhancement of teaching.

Granted, only rarely can a course transform a poor teacher into a great one. Yet if taken during those formative years of graduate study when individuals are most likely to welcome help, the advice provided can turn inaudible, unclear, or disorganized speakers into audible, clear, and organized ones. Most important, it can turn thoughtless teachers into thoughtful ones, a crucial step on the path to greater success in the classroom.

One final note. At the undergraduate institutions where our students went to teach, departmental chairs reported how well the instructors were performing and urged us to continue our efforts to enhance pedagogical skills. Sad to say, however, most members of our doctoral program were focused only on increasing research productivity and believed time spent on improving teaching could be more productively used trying to prepare articles for publication. Hence, when I retired, the practicum was abandoned, and as a result the undergraduate departmental chairs began to criticize our students' inadequate performance in the classroom.

Not surprisingly, such complaints went unheeded.

# Chapter 4

# EXAMINATIONS

As I MENTIONED EARLIER, the practicum covered the topic of examinations, an unhappy subject for both students and teachers. For students, exams are the stuff of nightmares; for teachers, they result in stacks of papers requiring correction and grading. Thus the question arises: Why not dispense with tests?

The answer is that, carefully prepared, they serve important purposes. First, an exam provides the opportunity for students to discover the scope and depth of their understanding. To speak glibly about a subject is not nearly as indicative of one's knowledge as to reply without prompting to pertinent questions and commit those answers to paper for scrutiny.

Students, though, are not the only ones evaluated by exams. Another purpose they serve is providing teachers with the opportunity to assess the effectiveness of their instruction. Analyzing test results allows teachers to learn how they have succeeded and where they have failed.

An additional value to examinations is the time spent preparing for them. Because questions are not known beforehand, students need to undertake a thorough study of all the material and anticipate what may be asked. In doing so, they are led to analyze and synthesize the subject, thereby enhancing their mastery of it.

Term papers have their own worth but are not substitutes for an examination. In researching papers, students need learn about only those parts of the course bearing directly on the chosen topic. Suppose you are studying the American political system and are asked to learn the roles of the executive, legislative, and judicial branches of the United States government. If you write a term paper on the Department of Education, you may do so without acquiring knowledge of much of the course material. Only an examination will cover all the ground.

Consider the example of a student who came to see me after receiving a C on her test. She was disappointed, especially because, as she explained, she had always been an A student. I asked whether she had studied as hard for this exam as for previous ones, and to my surprise she told me that she had never before taken an examination. She had gone to a secondary school where tests were considered outmoded, then her first two collegiate years were spent at a school that had substituted term papers for exams. I asked whether she thought her learning had been helped or hindered by their absence. She replied that until then she had always thought that avoiding tests had been to her advantage, but she now realized that her grasp of material had been flimsy. She had never learned a body of material thoroughly enough to draw on it at will and utilize it effectively whenever needed. In short, she never had received the benefits of studying for an exam.

But if examinations are so beneficial, what are the arguments against them?

First, some say that exams do not provide a sound basis for evaluating a student's achievement. After all, they require that one demonstrate knowledge under challenging conditions, answering a restricted set of questions within a limited time, thus causing pressure that prevents many from doing their best work.

This line of argument, however, overlooks that stress exists whenever anyone attempts to prove competence to specialists. For example, a violinist feels pressure when auditioning for an orchestral position. Tension is inherent in such situations because experts have high standards that are challenging to meet, and you need to do so at an appointed time. The golfer who appears skillful in practice but plays poorly on the course lacks effective control of the requisite skills. Similarly, students who sound informed in conversation but perform poorly in exams lack command of the subject. Thus examination pressure does not invalidate but rather confirms the significance of the results.

A second criticism is that exams inhibit students' independence, discouraging them from pursuing their own interests and instead imposing the study of materials chosen by the instructor.

Why assume, though, that mastering a subject involves only learning those aspects you happen to find interesting? For example, to grasp American history involves studying all periods, not just the Civil War or the New Deal. You may not be interested in the colonial age, but if you claim expertise in American history, you are expected to be familiar with it all, and the teacher is your guide to comprehending the subject fully. Doing so is not limiting but liberating, removing barriers to understanding and making possible more independent thinking.

A final criticism of examinations is that they stifle creativity, emphasizing the mindless reiteration of facts instead of encouraging imaginative thinking. Examinations are said to impede rather than promote learning.

But this line of attack is mistaken for two reasons. First, only poor examinations emphasize learning by rote. Good ones place familiar material in a somewhat unfamiliar light and lead students to make valuable connections in their thinking.

Second, the mastery of any field requires control of relevant information and skills. As Alfred North Whitehead wrote, "There is no getting away from the fact that things have been found out, and that to be effective in the modern world you must have a store of definite acquirement of the best practice. To write poetry you must study metre: and to build bridges you must be learned in the strength of material. Even the Hebrew prophets had learned to write, probably in those days requiring no mean effort. The untutored art of genius is—in the words of the Prayer Book—a vain thing, fondly invented."[1]

---

1. Alfred North Whitehead, *The Aims of Education and Other Essays* (1929; New York: Free Press, 1967), 34.

Imaginative thinking does not flow from those ignorant of fundamental information, and examinations reveal whether you know the basics. Hence testing, rather than stifling creativity, provides a framework in which it can flourish.

In the practicum we discussed these matters, then students constructed examinations and received comments from one another, pointing out questions that were especially effective as well as those that were ambiguous or repetitive. After this exercise, students were more likely to take examinations seriously and be aware of how to construct them appropriately.

*Chapter 5*

# GRADES

ANOTHER CRITICAL SUBJECT WE discussed in the practicum was grading.

After all, many teachers are uncomfortable with grades, viewing them as inherently inaccurate devices that, in attempting to measure people, only traumatize and dehumanize them. This concern, however, is a tangle of misconceptions.

A grade represents an expert's judgment of the quality of a student's work in a specific course. As such, it can serve not only to determine whether students are making satisfactory progress or earning academic honors but also to aid students themselves in judging their past efforts and formulating their future plans.

Would these functions be better served if, as some have suggested, grades were replaced by letters of evaluation? In addition to the impracticality of a professor's writing hundreds of individual comments and evaluators reading thousands, the value of such letters would be severely limited if they didn't include specific indications of students' level of performance—in other words, grades. Otherwise, the letters would be more likely to reveal the teachers' literary styles than the students' academic accomplishments. Remarks one instructor considers high praise may be used indiscriminately by another, while comments intended as mild commendation might be mistaken for tempered criticism.

While a piece of work would not necessarily be graded identically by all specialists, those in the same department usually agree whether a student's performance has been outstanding, good, fair, poor, or unsatisfactory, the levels of achievement typically symbolized by A through F. Granted, experts sometimes disagree, but in doing so they do not obliterate the distinction between their knowledgeable judgments and a novice's uninformed impressions.

What of the oft-repeated charge that grades are impersonal devices that reduce people to letters of the alphabet? That criticism is misguided. A grade is not a measure of a person but of a person's level of achievement in a particular course. A student who receives a grade of C in introductory French is not a C person with a C personality or C moral character but one whose performance in introductory French was acceptable but not distinguished. Perhaps the student will do much better in later courses and may eventually excel in the study of French literature, but this first try was not highly successful.

Whether grades are fair, however, depends on a teacher's conscientiousness in assigning them, a point I stressed in the practicum. One potential misuse is to award grades on bases other than a student's level of achievement. Irrelevant criteria include a student's gender, race, nationality, physical appearance, dress, personality, attitudes, innate capacities, and previous academic record. None of these factors should even be considered in deciding a student's grade. Performance in the course should be the only criterion.

If an A in symbolic logic indicates that the student tried hard, came from an impoverished community, or displayed an ingratiating personality, then the A would be hopelessly ambiguous and serve no purpose. If, on the other hand, the grade signifies that the student has a firm grasp of the essentials of symbolic logic, then the message is clear.

The most effective means for ensuring that no extraneous factors enter grading is for the instructor to clarify at the beginning of the term how final grades will be determined. How much will the final examination count? How about the papers and other short assignments? Will the student's participation be a factor? Answering these questions at the outset enables students to concentrate their energies on the most important aspects of the course, not waste time speculating about the instructor's intentions.

Yet if the announced system is unnecessarily complicated, it can distort the purpose of the course. In the practicum, as part of an exercise in constructing a syllabus, students were asked to present a system of grading. One enthusiastic participant proposed something along these lines: To receive an A you need to accumulate 965 points out of 1000, and the final exam is worth 350, each of the other two exams is worth 120, each of the two papers is worth 140, and class discussion is worth 130. As the group pointed out and the student quickly agreed, his proposal had taken on the appearance of a complicated game show. Instead, the rule of thumb should be: Explain your grading but keep matters simple.

We also explored the most common misuses of grades. One I especially warned against is the practice commonly referred to as "grading on a curve." The essence of this scheme is for the instructor to decide before the course begins what percentage of students will receive each grade. This method will produce aesthetically pleasing designs on a graph but is nevertheless conceptually confused. While a student's achievement should be judged in the light of reasonable expectations, these do not depend on such haphazard circumstances as the mix of students taking the course concurrently.

Consider the plight of a student who earns an 80 on an exam but receives a D because most classmates scored higher. Yet the following semester in the same course, another earns an 80 with the same answers and receives an A because this time almost all classmates scored lower. Two students, identical work, different grades: the system is patently unfair.

Years ago I overheard a student complain to his instructor about receiving a B. This nationally known scholar responded sympathetically but explained with regret that all the A's had been taken. His scholarly skills far exceeded his pedagogical wisdom.

Why do so many instructors resort to this approach? By so doing they avoid responsibility for determining the level of work each grade represents. They are also free to construct examinations without concern for skewed results, because even if the highest grade is 30 out of 100, grading on a curve will yield apparently acceptable consequences. Yet the appearance is deceiving because class rank will have been conflated with subject mastery. The Procrustean practice of grading on a curve rests on this muddle and should be abandoned (although inept teaching or badly constructed examinations should not result in unconscionably low grades).

A different distortion of the grading system, rare today, is an unwillingness to award high grades. Instructors who adopt this attitude take pride in rigor. But just as a third-grade student who receives an A in mathematics need not be the equal of Isaac Newton, so a first-year college student may receive an A in writing without being the equal of George Orwell. Receiving an A only means that, judged by reasonable standards, the student has done excellent work. An instructor who rarely rewards high grades is failing to distinguish good from poor performance. Doing so does not uphold academic standards but only misinterprets the grading symbols, thereby undermining their appropriate functions.

A more common misuse of the grading system is the reluctance to award low grades, a practice popularly known as "grade inflation." It results from the unwillingness of instructors to give students the bad news that they have not done as well as they might have hoped. Yet maintaining academic standards rests on the willingness of professors to tell the truth.

Understandably, some are concerned about the possible injustice of giving their own students realistic grades while other students receive inflated ones. The solution adopted at some colleges is for transcripts to include not only a student's course grade but also the average grade for all those in the course. In this way grade inflation is exposed and unfairness dissipated. In any case, each instructor who inflates grades adds to the problem.

Awarding grades also calls for a sense of fair play. Consider a teacher I knew who gave relatively easy exams throughout the semester, thereby leading students to believe they were doing well. The final examination, however, was vastly more difficult, and many students were shocked and angered to receive low grades for the course. Clearly, this instructor misled and harmed his students; he was akin to a storeowner who announces a major sale but fools customers by applying low prices to only a few rarely sought items. After all, ethics applies not only to physicians, nurses, lawyers, business managers, journalists, and engineers but also to teachers. They, too, can lie, mislead, and fail to fulfill all manner of professional responsibilities. Indeed, classrooms are no more free of misconduct than hospitals, courts, or boardrooms.

Grading is especially sensitive to mishandling because assessments are done privately and results are not easily challenged. Teachers, therefore, need to make every effort to treat students equitably.

Few professors have ever spent time discussing fair grading practices, yet students care deeply about the matter. A practicum can provide a convenient setting for considering the numerous issues that surround a teacher's responsibility to provide appropriate assessment.

*Chapter 6*

# A Teacher's Role

A PRACTICUM ALSO AFFORDS an opportunity for future teachers to consider how they should relate to students. Here a variety of moral issues arise.

A key principle is that teachers cannot avoid responsibility for guiding the learning process. They should be expected to know which material is to be studied and in what order it is best presented. They should also understand how a student can proceed most productively, what constitutes individual progress, and when someone has achieved it.

Suppose you enroll in an introductory course in chess and your instructor begins by inquiring whether the class would prefer to learn first how rooks move or when castling is permitted. Such a question would be senseless, for a reasonable answer depends on some knowledge of chess, and if you already had that, you wouldn't be in a class for beginners.

As teachers are appropriately held responsible for what occurs in the classroom, so with responsibility goes authority. We speak not only of authority as power but also of an authority, that is, an expert. The two concepts are related: The responsibilities that entail the exercise of authority or power are typically assigned to individuals by virtue of their presumed authority or expertise.

Such is the case with teachers, for their superior knowledge justifies their being assigned pedagogic responsibilities. After all, if teachers understand a subject no better than their students, why should students be charged tuition while teachers receive paychecks? I have heard teachers minimize their own importance and emphasize how much they have learned from their students, but I have yet to hear a single professor offer to exchange an instructor's salary for a student's bill.

To recognize a teacher's authority, however, is not to suggest that the teacher should act in an authoritarian manner. The appropriate relationship is that of guide, not god. Guides are expected to be familiar with the areas through which they lead you, pointing out highlights and warning of dangers. They are to blame if you follow their instructions but miss important sites or fall victim to a peril that should have been anticipated. The guide who responds to charges of incompetence by blaming the visitors' lack of knowledge is not thereby relieved of responsibility.

Recognizing the extent to which students are necessarily dependent on their instructors leads to the realization of how much damage faculty members can inflict. Which of us has not felt the sting of a teacher's thoughtless gibe? Or been victimized by carelessness or meanness? Or developed an aversion to some subject as a result of a teacher's incompetent presentation? In short, the teacher has the capacity to help or harm students. Achieving the former and avoiding the latter are the primary responsibilities of every instructor.

Another moral issue is failing to treat all students with equal concern. The temptation for most teachers is to seek satisfaction by focusing on the more accomplished members of the class. The aim of teaching, however, is not to please teachers but to enlighten students. Although some are difficult to reach, all who are trying to learn should be offered help in doing so.

The challenge of effective teaching is more than encouraging the eager and gifted. Rather, a critical concern is appealing to those who arrive with little interest and seemingly limited talent. Can they be excited about the material and inspired to enhance their knowledge and skills?

I should add that a concern for all students is compatible with giving attention to the strongest, perhaps by offering them in-class challenges or extra-credit assignments. In truth, though, the gifted do not require far more regard than others. Do you suppose Plato was especially worried whether he could keep the interest of his student Aristotle?

A different challenge is presented by a student who is emotionally unstable. In that case teachers, however well-intentioned, should not try to practice clinical psychology. Rather, those students should be advised to visit the school's counseling service where professionals are qualified to deal with such matters.

Yet the most egregious instances of professorial malfeasance rest on the mistaken supposition that teachers ought to be friends with their students. What is wrong with this approach, as Sidney Hook pointed out, is that "teachers must be friendly without becoming a friend, although [they] may pave the way for later friendship, for friendship is a mark of preference and expresses itself in indulgence, favors, and distinctions that unconsciously find an invidious form."[1] Faculty ought to care about the progress of each student, but they should remain dispassionate, able to deliberate, judge, and act without thought of personal interest or advantage. Even the appearance of partiality is likely to impair the learning process by damaging an instructor's credibility, causing doubt that standards are being applied fairly.

Every instructor should scrupulously avoid giving preferential treatment. If one student is permitted to write a paper instead of taking an examination, that option should be available to everyone in the class. If one is allowed to turn in an assignment late, then all others in like circumstances should be offered the same opportunity. And if one is invited to the professor's home for dinner, then everyone should receive similar invitations. Adherence to this guideline never leads to trouble; breaking it is often problematic.

---

1. Sidney Hook, *Education for Modern Man: A New Perspective* (1963; Eugene, OR: Wipf and Stock Publishers, 2020), 230–231.

One obvious implication of the principle of equal consideration is that between teacher and student not only is friendship inappropriate but even more so is romance. Even if a student never enrolls in a professor's classes, their liaison suggests that this faculty member does not view students from a professional standpoint. If an attempt is made to keep the relationship secret, the professor's integrity is compromised. In any case, such efforts at concealment almost always fail, thus besmirching the professor's reputation for honesty.

Should a student seek to initiate an affair with a professor, the only proper response is an unequivocal refusal. On the other hand, for a professor to attempt to seduce or coerce a student is an egregious abuse of authority that provides strong grounds for dismissal.

When a student has left the college or moved to a different unit of the university, whatever personal contact may develop with a professor is up to the two of them. During the years of undergraduate or graduate study, however, the only appropriate relationship is professional. To maintain these bounds is in everyone's best interest, and no more so than in the context of scholarly collaboration.

For whatever reasons, academics have recently had a plethora of scandals involving forms of sexual harassment and abuse. Under these unfortunate circumstances, teachers should be especially vigilant to maintain their proper function as guides through a field of study. They should not seek or accept the role of psychiatrist, friend, or lover.

To summarize the value of a graduate school practicum, it offers a remedy for the all-too-common situation in which instructors begin teaching without any guidance in conducting a class, constructing examinations, awarding grades, or relating to students. No wonder so many professors view themselves as researchers, not teachers. After all, if a graduate student is told nothing about a teacher's responsibilities, how important can they be?

## Chapter 7

# APPOINTMENTS

WHILE OFFERING A PRACTICUM would be a major step in enhancing teaching, also needed are adjustments in departmental policies regarding faculty appointments. Instituting these changes is my second suggestion.

From the outset of every search process, quality of instruction should be on everyone's mind. Indeed, when an opening is announced, the description of the position should stress the importance of excellence in teaching. At UVM, where decades ago I chaired a department that cared deeply about pedagogical matters, every position description included the words, "Excellence in research and teaching required."

All such announcements use the acronyms "AOS" and "AOC" to mean "areas of specialization" and "areas of competence." Candidates often wonder, though, how to draw the distinction. The practice should be that AOS denotes research interests, while AOC indicates teaching competencies. Applicants can thereby indicate not only their areas of research but also the courses they are prepared to teach.

An additional way to determine a candidate's teaching interests would be to follow the practice that was used at Vassar College when I was interviewed for my first full-time position. I was asked to examine the school's catalogue and indicate which courses I would prefer to teach, which I would be willing to teach, and which I would not want to teach. As I was told later, my candidacy was strengthened because the preferences I listed matched the department's instructional needs. In any case, the procedure indicated how seriously the department considered a candidate's teaching range.

Unfortunately, many departments proceed quite differently. Let me offer a fictional but realistic example. Imagine a music department that has four members teaching the history of Western music. Let us designate them as A, B, C, and D. A teaches Renaissance music, B the Baroque age, C the Classical period, and D the music of the 20th and 21st centuries. What's missing?

A neutral observer would immediately recognize a crucial gap: post-Beethoven music of the Romantic period, including such leading figures as Brahms and Wagner.

A candidate teaching the Romantic era, however, may not be the department's first priority. Consider how the discussion might proceed.

A. I'm supposed to cover all of Renaissance music, but my research focuses on the early period. We need someone for the late.

B. My work is centered on Bach, but there's so much more in the Baroque. Let's add someone who specializes in other Baroque composers. Nineteenth-century music is important, but I haven't heard much call from students wishing to specialize in Tchaikovsky or Verdi.

C. Recently I've been concentrating on Beethoven's quartets. How about someone whose research focuses on Haydn or Mozart? We can also use someone who is willing to cover the year-long survey in the history of music.

D. Contemporary music is so varied that we need another person to do it justice. I have a friend from graduate school who has published on electronic music and would be a terrific colleague.

The pattern is clear. Each member hopes to use the appointment to advance a personal research agenda. Here's commentary to help explain the exchange.

A. The Renaissance historian seeks a colleague with similar scholarly interests so as to have someone at hand for discussion and assistance. Rather than saying so, however, A stresses differences between the early and later Renaissance, then argues that the department needs a specialist in both. The problem is that any subject can be divided into smaller units and the argument made that each unit needs coverage. We might term this strategy "divide and augment." In a large department, multiple scholars for a single area may be reasonable, but this small program has room at most for only one course per year in Renaissance music.

B. The Baroque historian also uses the "divide and augment" strategy, followed by an appeal to lack of student interest in researching nineteenth-century music. But if Baroque music wasn't offered in the curriculum, would students complain about a lack of opportunity to focus on Corelli or Tartini?

C. The classical specialist seeks a colleague who specializes in Haydn or Mozart, as well as someone to teach the history of music survey that requires extensive preparation and covers materials outside any one instructor's scope. This professor proposes that department members avoid that demanding assignment by handing it to a newcomer who, perhaps without much enthusiasm but in an effort to gain the position, would be willing to offer the course.

D. The contemporary music scholar uses the "divide and augment" strategy, then adds what might be labelled the "I have a friend" approach. This maneuver typically leads a professor to overrate professional pals with whom they share research interests, then become angry if colleagues do not share this view.

Ultimately, whichever professor is politically savvy and most determined carries the day. In any case, the probability is high that the Romantic period will continue uncovered, and the most pliant member of the department will be dragooned into teaching the survey course.

To an outside observer, however, the sensible strategy would be to appoint a specialist in the Romantic era who is a strong teacher with broad interests, able to approach the survey course with inventiveness and zeal. The members of the department would undoubtedly grumble at this suggestion, given their lack of interest in the Romantic period. Indeed, they are likely to add that reports of teaching skill are unreliable.

Here they would have a point. After all, were a doctoral program to offer the sort of practicum I described earlier, the instructor would be in position to write a letter of recommendation that could provide insight into a candidate's teaching performance. In the absence of such a practicum, though, while a letter may contain a sentence praising a candidate's pedagogical skills, the author usually lacks evidence to support such an assessment. Here's a typical comment: "I am confident that Robin will be highly successful with students." If not based on classroom observation, such a remark is merely a hope and should be discounted.

In the absence of evidence about a candidate's teaching prowess, departments commonly request applicants to submit a statement describing their approach to teaching. This requirement is meant to suggest that the department cares about quality of instruction, but the practice makes as little sense as judging a candidate for an orchestral position as a cellist by reading the candidate's statement about playing the cello.

Obviously, we judge proficiency in action not by reading statements but by observing the skills in use. The critical test for teachers is not how they write or talk about teaching but how they teach.

Far more useful would be asking candidates to submit syllabi or examinations from courses they have taught or hoped to teach. Such documents would at least indicate how applicants plan a course, what readings they choose, what assignments they require, what sorts of exams they give, and how they grade students. Whether the course had been offered or only planned, such material would be informative.

Then at initial interviews, follow-up questions could be posed:

- Why did you choose that anthology rather than another?
- Why did you pick the topics you stressed?
- Why did you structure the exams as you did?

The answers would not reveal which candidates excelled in the classroom but would at least suggest how thoughtfully they approach their pedagogic responsibilities.

Eventually the department decides on a short list of candidates to be invited for campus visits. Too often these occasions consist of little more than a scholarly presentation, including a series of technical questions and answers, lunch with all interested members of the department at which a candidate's research program is explored, a quick chat with a dean, and farewells.

What should occur is quite different. Each candidate should be asked not only to give a research paper but also to prepare a talk on an elementary topic, organized and presented as if the audience were introductory students. In this test of pedagogic skills, candidates should be judged by their handling of the key elements of effective instruction: motivation, organization, and clarity. At UVM we required such a talk from each candidate, and the presentations were invariably reliable predictors of classroom success.

You might wonder how long into each talk it took for its quality to become obvious. You might suppose an hour would be needed or at least a half hour. One recent writer on college teaching doubts that an entire class, or even two, would enable the observer to "say anything meaningful or important" about the instruction.[1] In fact, rarely did it take more than ten minutes. Did the candidate

1. Jonathan Zimmerman, *The Amateur Hour: A History of College Teaching in America* (Baltimore: Johns Hopkins University Press, 2020), ix.

speak at an appropriate pace, make eye contact with the listeners, motivate interest in the issue, organize the subject, and ensure that the audience understood what was being said? If the answers were in the negative, the talk was a failure.

One brief story. During my time at UVM, the head of the philosophy department at a large state university asked me whether at my school, like his, enrollment in philosophy courses had been shrinking. I told him that, on the contrary, ours had been growing. He was amazed and wondered how I accounted for this phenomenon. "Excellent teaching," I said. "We try to make sure that all the candidates we appoint have the capacity for both outstanding research and outstanding teaching. What do you look for?"

"Fine scholars," he replied. "We wouldn't appoint anyone who hasn't delivered a paper to the department."

"Why not test their teaching, too?" I asked.

"Never thought of it," he muttered.

If a football franchise wishes to increase its team speed, the obvious step is to draft or trade for players who can run fast. If, instead, the team chooses players who are strong but slow, speed will continue to be a concern. Analogously, if a department seeks to enhance its enrollment, the obvious step is to choose applicants who excel in the classroom. If, instead, the department chooses scholars with little teaching skill, attracting students will continue to be a problem.

Ideally, those offered appointments should be outstanding scholars and teachers (later I'll discuss the component of service). Given the large numbers of applicants for every full-time position, finding those who are first-rate in both respects should not present an insuperable difficulty.

The key, however, is that when a decision is made on whom to appoint, quality of teaching is taken seriously. The wrong attitude would be expressed by members of a department who defended their choice as follows: "Smith is a terrific scholar who in time will become more adept at teaching." This judgment is no more convincing than saying, "Jones is a terrific teacher who in time will become more adept at research." Neither remark is plausible and should not carry the day.

New members of the faculty should understand that while they are permitted and even encouraged to visit classes taught by their more senior colleagues, veteran instructors will visit classes taught by newcomers. In all cases, the observer should sit in the back of the room and not take any role (participation impedes disinterested assessment) but afterwards discuss all aspects of the session: how a question was well put, how discussion may have gone off track, whether the instructor was audible, whether any technology was used effectively, how a difficult concept might have been presented more clearly, or how an idea explained in one context might have been applied in another. The aim is not to interfere with the instructor's distinctive teaching style but to enhance it. Outstanding scholars provide junior colleagues with support in their scholarly endeavors; similarly, top-notch teachers should aid junior colleagues in dealing with their pedagogic challenges. At UVM we had such a policy in place, and it worked remarkably well.

Admittedly, some professors are uncomfortable with colleagues sitting in their classes yet typically allow visits from auditors, friends or relatives of students, and even faculty members from other departments. Why, then, should doors be locked against those most qualified to understand what is going on? What would we think of surgeons who refused to allow their operations to be observed by other surgeons? Surely we would have little confidence in the skills of those who defended such a policy of secrecy. We should be equally dubious about the pedagogical proficiency of those who are uncomfortable if someone knowledgeable watches them teach.

The changes I have suggested are no panacea. Taken together, though, they enhance the importance of teaching and can quite easily be instituted by any department that cares about the matter. If more did, these policies would become commonplace.

*Chapter 8*

# Evaluating Teaching

Appropriate evaluation of teaching is a critical step toward enhancing its importance. At present, the common practice is judging an instructor's pedagogic skill primarily on the basis of student evaluations. Changing that system is my third suggestion.

The practice became widespread in the 1960s (although begun decades earlier) when enterprising undergraduates distributed light-hearted compilations of tips about the more and less effective members of the faculty, thereby aiding those registering for courses. A decade later these informal reactions had been transformed into complex statistics, obtained by formal procedures and relied on heavily by administrators to help decide an instructor's merit pay increases, reappointment, promotion, and tenure.

The rationale for instituting such a system was that when faculty fail to fulfill their obligations, students suffer the consequences. Shouldn't students, therefore, have a strong voice in evaluating faculty?

This line of reasoning is fallacious. When airplane pilots fail to fulfill their obligations, passengers often suffer the consequences, but passengers should not have a strong voice in evaluating pilots. A plane has a rough landing. Was the pilot at fault? Simply being a passenger does not enable one to know.

Some proponents of student ratings have argued that learners are the best evaluators of their own responses, drawing an analogy to the restaurant patron who is a better judge of the food than the chef. But while those who eat know how the food tastes, a nutritionist most reliably judges its nutritional benefit, just as educators most reliably judge educational value.

Students who by definition have not mastered the subject are poorly situated to judge how well it is being taught. Perhaps they find a concept challenging. Is the instructor to blame, or is the difficulty intrinsic to the material?

Granted, students are a convenient source for easily verifiable matters such as whether teachers hold class regularly, speak at an understandable pace, encourage class participation, maintain interest, return examinations without delay, provide detailed comments on term papers, appear at announced office hours, and so on. Students, however, are not in position to know whether faculty are knowledgeable or their presentations reliable.

Consider this question that appeared on a widely used evaluation form: "Does the instructor discuss recent developments in the field?" How are students expected to know the source of the information a teacher offers? Even if something is described to them as a recent development in the field, they are still in the dark as to whether that material is either recent or significant.

Some years ago an experiment was carried out under controlled conditions to test the hypothesis that learners can be seriously mistaken about their instructor's competence. A distinguished-looking professional actor with an authoritative manner (real name Michael Fox) was selected to present a lecture to several groups of educators. They were told they would be hearing a talk by Dr. Myron L. Fox, an expert on the application of mathematics to human behavior. His address was titled "Mathematical Game Theory as Applied to Physician Education." The actor was coached "to present his topic and conduct his question-and-answer period with an excessive use of double talk, neologies, non sequiturs, and contradictory statements. All this was to be interspersed with parenthetical and meaningless references to unrelated topics."

At the end of the one-hour lecture and subsequent half-hour discussion, a questionnaire inquired what the listeners thought of Dr. Fox. Here are some responses:

> Excellent presentation, enjoyed listening.
>
> Has warm manner. Good flow, seems enthusiastic.
>
> Lively examples. Extremely articulate.
>
> Good analysis of subject that has been personally studied before.
>
> He was certainly captivating. Knowledgeable.

My favorite reply was offered by one participant who found the presentation "too intellectual." Most important, many more responses were favorable than unfavorable, and not one listener saw through the hoax. The authors' concluded that "students' satisfaction with learning may represent little more than the illusion of having learned."[1]

Admittedly, student ratings yield quantifiable results that can easily be given the appearance of exactitude. For example, I have before me a computer-generated spreadsheet, typical of those provided each semester to faculty at many colleges. It indicates that in an English composition course, on a scale of a low of 1 to a high of 5, the instructor scored 4.85 for "Mastery of Subject," while the average for instructors for all sections of the course was 4.67; for all courses in the department, the average was 4.60; for all courses in the school it was 4.62. Sending such pseudo-precise data to faculty members with the understanding that their scores will play a significant role in personnel decisions is demeaning to all involved.

Furthermore, evaluating an instructor primarily on the basis of student opinion is not only inappropriate but also dangerous. As Charles Frankel observed, "Teaching is a professional relationship, not a popularity contest. To invite students to participate in the

---

1. Donald H. Naftulin, John E. Ware, Jr., and Frank A. Donnelly, "The Doctor Fox Lecture: A Paradigm of Educational Seduction," *Journal of Medical Education* 48 (1973) 630–635. An excerpt from the lecture is available on YouTube.

selection or promotion of their teachers . . . exposes the teacher to intimidation."[2] No professor should be put in a position in which advantage is gained by granting students favors in exchange for their support.

Admittedly, some educational researchers have concluded that student evaluations, viewed in proper perspective, can provide useful information. The crucial insight, however, supported by numerous studies, is that such evaluations always need to be considered in the context of peer evaluations. Otherwise, as one researcher found long ago and many others have since confirmed, institutions are "flying blind."[3]

Corporate executives judge other corporate executives to decide promotions in the company, and attorneys judge other attorneys to decide partnerships in the law firm. Likewise, professors should judge other professors to decide matters such as reappointment, promotion, and tenure. Indeed, no professionals should shirk the responsibility of judging their colleagues. To do so is not only inappropriate but inimical to the interests of those supposedly served. After all, if a quack is practicing surgery in a hospital, who is to blame, the patients or other physicians? If an incompetent is lecturing at a university, the ones at fault are not the students but the other professors. They are responsible for systematically observing classes and gaining insight into what is occurring.

Faculty rightfully claim authority in the academic sphere. When the time comes for evaluating teaching, they should not abandon their duty.

2. Charles Frankel, *Education and the Barricades* (New York: Norton, 1968), 30–31.

3. Charles B. Schultz, "Some Limits to the Validity and Usefulness of Student Rating of Teachers: An Argument for Caution," *Educational Research Quarterly* 3 (1978), 12–27.

*Chapter 9*

# TENURE

NONE OF THE SUGGESTIONS I have made thus far would fundamentally change academic culture unless quality of teaching plays a crucial role in tenure decisions. But what is the argument for maintaining the tenure system, how are tenure decisions presently made, and what adjustments are needed for quality of teaching to be given the weight it deserves? Answering those questions leads to my fourth suggestion.

When thinking about the centrality of tenure to faculty life, I always return to an image related by philosopher Andrew Oldenquist. He recalled that at his school, The Ohio State University, an art professor had placed in his studio window a small blue neon sign he had made that flashed "tenure." Oldenquist speculated, "Perhaps it counted as conceptual art; perhaps it won him tenure. I never knew."[1] Regardless, the sign serves as a striking reminder of an aspect of academic life that professors especially treasure.

Those who possess tenure hold lifetime appointments, revocable only in rare instances of gross incompetence or moral turpitude. Yet reference to this prerogative invariably gives rise to the same questions: Why should anyone receive permanent

---

1. Andrew Oldenquist, "Tenure: Academe's Peculiar Institution," in *Morality, Responsibility, and the University: Studies in Academic Ethics,* ed. Steven M. Cahn (Philadelphia: Temple University Press, 1990), 56.

job security? Doesn't tenure pamper the indolent and protect the incompetent?

Academic tenure is not as singular as often supposed. In most organizations of university size, employees, whether at lower ranks or in middle management, are rarely dismissed for cause. Due to poor performance they may be passed over for promotion, given lateral transfers, or occasionally demoted, but rarely are they discharged. While plant closings or fiscal crises may precipitate worker layoffs, tenured professors, too, face the loss of their positions if a department is phased out or a school closes.

Even the mechanics of the tenure system are hardly unique. Consider large law firms, which routinely recruit new associates with the understanding that after several years they will either be offered some variety of permanent position or required to depart. Colleges make similar arrangements with beginning faculty members.

Despite such analogies, however, tenure undoubtedly provides professors an unusual degree of latitude and security. They are privileged to explore any area of interest and proceed in whatever manner they wish. No one may dictate to them that certain subjects are taboo, that certain methods of inquiry are illegitimate, or that certain conclusions are unacceptable.

Tenure thus guarantees academic freedom, the right of all qualified persons to discover, teach, and publish the truth as they see it within their fields of endeavor. Where academic freedom is secure, students enter classrooms with the assurance that instructors are espousing their own beliefs, not mouthing some orthodoxy they have been programmed to repeat.

Although widely seen as valuable, academic freedom is threatened whenever anyone seeks to stifle free inquiry in the name of some cause that supposedly demands everyone's unthinking allegiance. Some, for example, have sought to have a school adopt an official stance on issues unrelated to its educational mission. Free inquiry, however, is impeded when certain opinions are officially declared false and others true. Colleges and universities are not established to inform the public where a majority of the faculty stands on any issue, whether mathematical, scientific, or political. Whether an argument for the existence of God is sound, or our government's foreign policy misguided, are matters for discussion, not decree.

Maintaining free inquiry requires that all points of view be entitled to a hearing. Unfortunately, some both inside and outside academia have occasionally attempted to interfere with the presentation of a campus speaker whose views they find unpalatable. Yet as the lecturer remains civil, no one at the school, whether professors, students, or administrators, should block any individual from expressing ideas, no matter how noxious they may be. The greater danger lies in stifling them, for when one person's opinion is silenced, no one else's may be uttered in safety.

But might academic freedom be preserved without tenure, perhaps by some form of multi-year contracts? The problem besetting any alternative scheme is that it could too easily be misused, opening faculty members to attack because of their opinions.

A key feature of the tenure system is that those who hold tenure in a department decide whether it should be granted to others. Thus those who judge are not facing a conflict of interest, because their own tenure is not at stake. In any system of multi-year contracts, however, the question arises: Who should decide whether a contract ought to be renewed? If the decision is placed in the hands of other tenured professors, they would be voting while realizing that their own contracts would eventually come up for renewal. The result would be a conflict of interest. After all, if I support you, will you support me? Worse, the decision might be made by administrators with an ax to grind, favoring professors who have supported administrative initiatives. Such a system would produce an atmosphere of suspicion and recrimination, antithetical to independent thinking.

Unquestionably, the tenure system has dangers, but none as great as those that would attend its abandonment. To adapt a remark about democracy offered by Winston Churchill, tenure may be the worst system ever devised, except for all the others.

To defend the tenure system in principle, however, is not to applaud all the ways it has been implemented. Without doubt, many departments have supported candidates too liberally. Instead of individuals being required to demonstrate why they deserve tenure, a department has been expected to demonstrate why they don't. In court a person ought to be presumed not guilty until the evidence shows otherwise, but in matters of special skill you ought not be supposed qualified until so proven. A school's failure to observe this guideline results in a faculty encumbered with deadwood, and more than a few departments suffer from this unfortunate phenomenon.

Yet tenure decisions can present difficult problems and have been known to cause hostilities that last for decades. Unpleasant as events may become, though, faculty members need to act conscientiously because the future of their departments may be at stake. Even a single ill-advised decision may lead to years of disruption and possibly decay, bringing tenure itself into disrepute and thereby threatening that academic freedom the system is intended to preserve. In short, wise choices are a blessing, foolish ones a blight.

But what are the appropriate criteria for tenure decisions? Traditionally, three aspects of a faculty member's record are considered: scholarship, service, and teaching.

As to scholarship, it is widely recognized as an arduous undertaking. It requires not only engaging in research but publishing the results in scholarly articles and books. Even reading papers at professional conferences, while commendable, is insufficient because a scholar's original thinking needs to be available for scrutiny by experts, and the easiest way for them to have access is for material to be published. Scholarly writing need not be elegant (it rarely is), but it is required to be precise. Scholars cannot merely approximate the views they are trying to express; what they say needs to be formulated exactly.

Work counts most heavily if it is subject to peer review. University presses typically require that manuscripts be approved by at least two outside experts, and scholarly journals depend on evaluations by at least a couple of scholars, typically using "blind review," in which the evaluator does not know the identity of the author.

An article in a popular magazine is not equivalent to one accepted in a refereed journal. The local newspaper may request a professor's thoughts on events of the day, but no other scholars have examined the ideas to determine if they merit publication. A professor may even publish a best-selling book, but assuming that it has not been peer reviewed, it will be given far less weight than if it had been published by a relatively minor university press that relies on the judgments of experts.

As for the criterion of service, it typically involves participation in departmental committees, such as those overseeing the curriculum, student awards, library holdings, and so on. Other activities might be serving on a faculty-wide committee dealing with curricular and degree requirements, helping the admissions office by evaluating applications, lecturing to a campus group, or representing the school at a national conference. In any case, each member of a department is expected to assume a fair share of the day-to-day tasks that are an inescapable part of academic life.

Service, however, is not afforded the importance given to research, a disparity apparent in the methods by which each is evaluated. In the case of research, an elaborate review is undertaken, including faculty members reading the candidate's research as well as sending it out for judgments by experts in the field. In the case of service, the activities are merely listed on an individual's record; quantity is noted, whereas quality is rarely of concern.

Teaching is the third criterion in a tenure decision, and here we arrive at the crux of the problem. Teaching should be judged with the same care as research but too often is treated more like service.

If teaching were taken more seriously, evaluating it would involve input from departmental colleagues who would visit the professor's classes and assess syllabi, examinations, and test papers to evaluate teaching performance. Indeed, an outsider or two, experienced in evaluating teachers, might be asked to attend a couple of classes and write reviews.

Instead, courses an individual has taught are merely listed and supplemented by packets of student evaluations. The issue is not whether the professor excelled in the classroom but whether the performance was so subpar that it causes concern.

To see how tenure decisions should be made, consider two hypothetical cases, then three factual ones. Taken together, they clarify the importance of appropriate balancing of criteria.

Imagine that Adam comes to Eastern College to begin a professorial career. During his first two years, he gains experience teaching standard departmental offerings while struggling with and finally finishing his dissertation, which he and his advisor had optimistically estimated he would complete before his arrival. In his third and fourth years he devotes himself to planning several new courses and participating in an exciting multidisciplinary program. While reasonably successful as a teacher, he publishes two articles derived from his dissertation. In his fifth and sixth years he continues to enjoy rapport with students while publishing a couple of book reviews and another article, this one based on a seminar paper written in graduate school. He has also begun work on what he hopes will be a book-length manuscript, but the project is still at an early stage.

In his sixth year, in accordance with the principles of the American Association of University Professors, a decision needs to be made on Adam's tenure. He is liked by his students, has various publications, and is at work on a major scholarly project. He is a cooperative colleague and has participated enthusiastically in multidisciplinary activities. Should he be awarded tenure?

Doing so involves excessive risk, for Adam's most productive years may lie behind him. He has not demonstrated the capacity for sustained, creative effort, and a careful examination of his bibliography raises serious doubts whether he has produced any significant scholarship since his dissertation. His good rapport with students may be based more on a beginner's enthusiasm and spirit of camaraderie, possibly short-lived, rather than on fundamental pedagogic skills and enduring qualities of mind that would sustain his teaching in later years. Peer review, if used, may even have raised some doubts in this direction. His contributions to the life of the school may decline when the novelty of such activity wanes, and in time he may no longer be familiar with the frontiers of his own field. If he is awarded tenure, then fulfills our worst fears, those who suffer most will be the generations of students forced to endure his premature academic senility.

Admittedly, were he retained he might in the long run prove a significant asset to the college. That outcome, though, is only a possibility, not a probability. For the sake of future students as well as in the interest of each academic discipline, every effort should be made to appoint and retain only those individuals who, compared to all other available candidates, are most likely to achieve excellence. Adhering to such a rigorous standard is the surest way to avoid the succession of egregious and irremediable errors that are the likely consequences of laxity.

Adam's supporters, however, can be depended on to argue that the evaluations of his record have placed too much emphasis on the criterion of publication. After all, they may remind us, one great teacher wrote nothing: Socrates. Those who appeal to his case tend to overlook that the Athenian gadfly spent his life in public debate, befuddling the cleverest minds of his time, forcing them to rethink their fundamental commitments. Few would doubt the scholarly qualifications of any professor who could do the same. But as Socrates himself pointed out, impressing students and friends is no guarantee of one's acumen.

Adam's advocates will claim that despite his thin publication record, he has proven himself a good teacher. But is he merely competent, or is he so outstanding that we have strong reason to suppose that replacing him in the classroom would significantly reduce the quality of instruction? Unless the latter were the case, an individual should be appointed in his stead who would at least match him as a teacher while surpassing him as a scholar. After all, why should a college award tenure to a present member of the faculty if other persons more capable stand ready to serve?

In the face of this challenge, Adam's defenders are apt to retreat to the view that, while his credentials are admittedly borderline, we ought nevertheless give him the benefit of the doubt, taking into account the extra hours he has spent with students, the favors he has done for colleagues, and, above all, the disturbance and distress a rejection would cause him.

Those responsible for tenure decisions should never succumb to such pleadings; they are obliged to remember Sidney Hook's observation that "most . . . tenured faculty who have lapsed into apparent professional incompetence . . . were marginal cases when their original tenure status was being considered, and reasons other than their proficiency as scholars and teachers were given disproportionate weight."[2] The principle should be "when in doubt, say no," a policy that will not be popular with Adam, his family, or his friends. But only by maintaining rigorous standards for the awarding of tenure can an institution safeguard its academic quality.

Adam's record might be summarized as follows: good but not excellent teaching, good but not excellent service, and fair scholarship. This record does not justify the granting of tenure.

Consider next Eve, who begins her teaching career at Western University. Her dissertation, completed prior to her arrival, is published by a leading university press. Throughout the next five years, she contributes substantial articles to major professional journals, and months before she is to be considered for tenure, another major academic publisher accepts her second book.

Yet her teaching record is far less successful. Students complain that her lectures are bewildering and that she is rarely available for consultation outside class. Registration for her courses is small, although a few advanced students have signed up repeatedly. Peer review, if in use, may have revealed that she speaks in a monotone while peering out the window. Her presentations reflect a firm grasp of the most recent literature but are convoluted and fail to motivate most students. She has reluctantly agreed to serve on several departmental committees but has little to say at the meetings. Should she be awarded tenure?

2. Sidney Hook, *Education and the Taming of* Power (LaSalle, IL: Open Court, 1973), 213.

Her teaching is not good, and her service unimpressive. How strong is her scholarship? If the evidence indicates that no one is available who matches the quality of her research, then she has a case to receive tenure. Her teaching nevertheless presents a serious problem. Perhaps she could work only with advanced students and not be placed in introductory courses. If, however, she cannot be trusted to be effective at any level, then awarding her tenure is irresponsible because even a university that puts the highest premium on research is obligated to provide students with competent instruction.

Her situation might be summarized as follows: research outstanding, teaching weak, and service unimpressive. Only if outside experts agree that she is a scholar of unquestionable national or international renown might she deserve to be granted tenure.

Here's a third case, and this one has a factual basis. Linda (a pseudonym) was a fine teacher with a thin record of publications. Her service, though, was extraordinary. She chaired innumerable department and school-wide committees, displaying tact and insight. She spent countless hours preparing reports, planning conferences, and developing curricula. In many ways she was the heart and soul of her department and a crucial member of the college faculty. She was universally admired. Should she have received tenure?

Her situation might be summarized as follows: research thin, teaching strong, and service extraordinary. A replacement could be found who would be more heavily published and perhaps equally adept in the classroom, but no applicant could be expected to display her skill and commitment in dealing with people as well as her dedication and success in contributing to the welfare of her department and university.

In fact, she was denied tenure. I believe that decision was a mistake, and eventually her colleagues realized their error. By then, however, she had changed careers and climbed high on the corporate ladder.

Here's another actual case. The following account was authored by the late Paul J. Olscamp, a philosopher who served as president of Western Washington University (1975–1982), then of Bowling Green University (1982–1995). So far as I know, the narrative is factual, but I am not aware of who was involved or where the events occurred.

> Dr. Sally Morse (a fictitious name) found herself standing for tenure and promotion to associate professor. . . . Her department was targeted by her university as a "niche" discipline—a discipline or set of disciplines in a single department that the university wished to develop into a major player in the state's research environment. Expectations and rewards were higher for this department than for all others in the university. Morse submitted her application in her sixth year as a faculty member. Her teaching evaluations were excellent. She had few refereed publications, although the ones she had were in journals of high repute. Morse's service record was barely adequate, but the department informed the collegiate-level tenure and promotion committee that this was because the department discouraged her service activities and encouraged research in its place.
>
> Morse's research and publication record was clearly good enough to have earned her tenure in almost all of the university departments not designated as "niche." But it was average in comparison to the records of similar applicants from other "niche" programs. In a split vote within her department (6–4 with one abstention), she was recommended for tenure and promotion. Included in her file was a letter from the chair noting that Morse's research protocol was proceeding on schedule, and that the majority of the published work from her project could not be expected until her work was complete. It was also noted that Morse had not attracted significant outside funding from either government or private sources.
>
> On the basis of the department split vote, the collegiate-level tenure and promotion committee voted 5–4 to deny her tenure and promotion. The committee noted that this decision was particularly difficult for them because in most other departments her record would have qualified her for tenure and promotion. They also noted the systematic vagueness in the university's standards of

excellence with respect to the three evaluative criteria (teaching, research, and service).

The dean of the college recommended that Morse be given tenure but that promotion to associate professor be withheld pending further publication of her research. In his recommendation, the dean noted the split vote of the collegiate committee and their comments on the vagueness of the evaluative criteria. He stated that if "niche" programs were to have higher standards, then the departmental policies should say that and define them. The university-level tenure and promotion committee overturned the dean's recommendation, agreeing with the collegiate committee, but once again by a split vote, and with the same reservations expressed by the dean.

Olscamp now turns from factual description to an attempted justification of the ultimate decision.

It was clear that the expectations of Morse were much higher than the average for tenure and promotion applicants for the university as a whole. It was also clear that the higher criteria she had to meet were nowhere clearly defined in university policy. Given her record to date, it was reasonably foreseeable that Morse would continue to develop in her research, as well as in other professional categories.

Morse was a superstar teacher, and even in a niche department the school could not afford to lose such a fine instructor without violating its promises to students and their parents.

Olscamp concludes by sharing the outcome:

Dr. Sally Morse was given tenure and promoted . . . . The policies and procedures manuals were and are being revised to correct the deficiencies noted by the committees. The work is still in progress, having proven much more difficult than was anticipated.[3]

3. Paul J. Olscamp, *Moral Leadership: Ethics and the College Presidency* (Lanham, MD: Rowman & Littlefield, 2003), 43–47. The material has been edited for the sake of continuity.

The most noticeable feature of this case was Morse's weak support from her colleagues. In the absence of personal animosity, most departmental members are reluctant to deny tenure to colleagues with whom they have worked closely for years. In this case, however, only six out of eleven supported Morse. The college-level tenure and promotion committee voted against tenure, as is uncommon, and the Dean clearly had doubts, recommending tenure but not promotion, an unusual procedure because the two usually go together. The university-level tenure and promotion committee also voted against tenure, thereby overturning the dean's recommendation, a rare occurrence. As for Morse's research, although she was informed at the outset that it should be her first priority, she had few publications and did not attract outside funding, an important criterion for success in most science and some social science departments. That her record was good enough compared to members of other departments is irrelevant because those faculty were not provided with the support she had received.

Regarding her teaching, she received excellent student evaluations, but why did those qualify her as a "superstar" teacher? Apparently no peer evaluations were used. Furthermore, how many teachers received equally strong evaluations? Would someone else teaching her classes significantly reduce quality of instruction? If not, she could be replaced by someone who would at least match her as a teacher while surpassing her in scholarly output. Remember that for every opening hundreds of applications are received, and retaining her was preventing numerous others from being considered.

In addition, her service was described as "barely adequate," but that failing was excused because she was supposed to focus on research. Yet service can take various forms, many of which are not especially time-consuming, and her not finding some way to help her colleagues was a mark against her.

Olscamp presents the case for awarding her tenure, but to my mind his arguments fall short. He claims that her research would develop and might in the long run yield publications, but who knows? If those being considered for tenure do not publish when the pressure to do so is greatest, why assume they will do so when the strongest incentive has been removed? He also stresses that criteria for tenure in niche departments were not given with specificity, but he does not say that the situation differed in other departments. In fact, whenever experts assess quality, no simple formula can replace human judgment. Whether a pianist deserves a prize at a music competition or a movie is worthy of an award at a film festival is a decision that goes beyond mere numbers, and the same is the case for granting tenure. No wonder that, as Olscamp relates, the attempt to revise the policies and procedures manual proved much more difficult than anticipated. I doubt the work was ever completed.

The strangest aspect of the case is that Morse was ultimately awarded tenure not because of any scholarly contribution but because of her supposed status as a "superstar" teacher. Her performance in the classroom may have fit that description, yet Olscamp offers no evidence beyond excellent student evaluations. Were her colleagues impressed by observing her teaching or at least hearing her present lectures? Was registration in all her courses consistently massive? Did she win any teaching awards? If the case for her tenure depended on her supposedly offering superb instruction, why wasn't more done to assess it?

Extraordinary performance as a teacher can justify the awarding of tenure, but the case has to be overwhelming. Morse's was not; here's one that was.

Beginning in the 1960s, Robert Gurland taught philosophy at NYU. He published little, and while at the request of administrators he spoke to many university and outside groups, he was not active on departmental or schoolwide committees. Yet while his colleagues would teach ten or twenty students in a course, he would, no matter the subject, always teach over two hundred. On the first day of registration, his classes filled, and the demand invariably far exceeded the number of available seats. Students, regardless of their gender, race, ethnicity, or level of sophistication, flocked to his classes. He reciprocated the students' passion by knowing the name of everyone in every class, learning something about each, and personally grading, with numerous detailed comments, every one of the hundreds of papers.

He welcomed colleagues to observe his classes even without giving him prior notice, and, in light of the skepticism of some about the source of his popularity, he invited anyone who wished to review the exams he gave, the answer booklets his students submitted, and the grades he awarded (which were not especially generous). All who watched him teach and scrutinized the written record came away impressed. He taught virtually every course in the curriculum, from epistemology to ethics, from symbolic logic to medieval philosophy, from existentialism to the philosophy of sport. No area of the subject was outside his purview, and occasionally he created courses when a new area of the subject developed.

Admittedly, he had a most engaging personality, a wonderful sense of humor, and an unusual background that included stints as a minor league baseball player and a professional trumpeter in leading jazz bands, as well as having had extensive experience teaching mathematics and science in elementary school, junior high school, and high school.

On one occasion when I asked him to explain his remarkable success, he opened his battered briefcase and held up stacks of yellow pads filled with writing. He explained that these were his lectures, and although he never looked at them during his classes, he knew exactly what material he was going to cover and how it would be presented. Even his vivid examples were written down. In short, his seemingly freewheeling style was carefully planned.

He won teaching awards at a variety of levels and institutions, but such honors meant far less to him than the enthusiastic response of his students. They included many of the school's best undergraduates, a number of whom, influenced by him, became highly successful philosophy professors. Occasionally he taught at West Point. There he was such a hit with the cadets that he was offered a permanent position but turned it down to remain at NYU.

His situation might be summarized as follows: publications weak, service limited, and teaching on the highest possible level. Had he been replaced, the department could no doubt have found a stronger researcher who would have offered more consistent service on committees, but the quality of his teaching could not have been matched or even approached. Had he been replaced, student registration in the department would have plummeted, because he taught a massive percentage of all the students taking philosophy courses.

To no one's surprise, he received tenure. Generations of students were the beneficiary of that wise decision.

As an outstanding researcher may be awarded tenure even with a weak performance in the classroom, so tenure should also be available to an outstanding teacher with a thin record of research. Granted, the ideal candidate excels as both researcher and teacher, but just as an occasional exception is made so as not to lose a researcher of national stature, an occasional exception should also be made so as not to lose a teacher of extraordinary accomplishment.

Few teachers can attain such a level of excellence; after all, taking the lead in developing a new multidisciplinary program, teaching a single course that invariably has a high enrollment, offering extra help to struggling students, or attracting crowds to office hours does not by itself overcome a thin record of research. Nevertheless, a faculty member with a superlative record of teaching, unlikely to be matched by any possible replacement, should be considered a strong candidate for a tenured appointment.

Note that a corollary of serious evaluation of teaching is the willingness to differentiate among levels of effectiveness. We recognize the difference between research that is weak, mediocre, strong, or superb; the same distinctions apply to teaching. Not every accomplished researcher is a serious candidate for a Nobel Prize or its equivalent; neither is every sound teacher a serious candidate for the Teaching Hall of Fame.

Describing all teachers as "good" or "not so good" is a sign that teaching is not taken seriously. An individual may be said to be a good teacher, but "how good?" is a key question.

In sum, if the case for tenure relies heavily on meeting only one of the three criteria, that category needs to be filled in spectacular fashion. If the case depends heavily on only two of the criteria, then they should both be filled with unquestionable excellence. If the case depends, as most do, on meeting each of the three criteria, then they should all be filled with high quality. Anything less or even borderline, and the department should begin a new appointment process.

Finally, let me mention an alternative approach to granting tenure that some find appealing. I refer to the proposal to create two sorts of professorships: one in research and one in teaching. Then the criteria for tenure in the two cases would be vastly different.

I do not favor this idea. The motto "publish or perish" may not appeal to some, but few who oppose it would object to the demand that faculty "think or perish"; yet to publish is to make available to all the results of one's best thinking. Professors who fail to do so should be expected to seek alternative ways of providing substantial evidence of their intellectual vigor. If they are unable to shoulder the burden of proof, others are justified in doubting the quality of their thinking and hence their teaching.

As for those who excel in scholarship, they should be encouraged to communicate their insights in a classroom. A professor, as the word's medieval Latin origin *professare* suggests, is one who makes open declarations. Taking the time to motivate, organize, and clarify one's thinking so as to share it with others never harmed anyone and can help students, who, after all, contribute to supporting the professor's way of life.

Instituting two classes of instructors would not enhance but diminish the importance of teaching, suggesting that it is not an activity worth the time and effort of prestigious professors. That message is surely the wrong one.

## Chapter 10

# THE ADMINISTRATION

WHEREAS ANY INDIVIDUAL DEPARTMENT could implement my suggestions for offering a practicum, changing departmental practices, and relying on peer review, the criteria for deciding tenure cases involves the support of the administration because tenure is not awarded by a department but by a school.

The question then arises as to how to transform the way administrators view teaching. Taking appropriate steps to do so is my fifth and final suggestion. Some deans or provosts might be persuaded to change policies by pleas from strong departments or influential faculty members. In practice, however, turnover in these administrative posts occurs quite frequently, and searches for successors provide an excellent opportunity, perhaps the best, to push for policy changes. (Because many, although not all, presidents have limited participation in the inner workings of academia, focusing instead on the school's relationships with alumni, community, and government, in what follows I shall not refer to their role.)

Regardless of the school, the steps taken in any search for a senior academic administrator are remarkably similar. A search committee is formed, an advertisement is placed, a hundred or so applications are received, the list is shortened, letters of reference are obtained, another cut is made, campus interviews are conducted, the committee makes its recommendations, and a high-ranking official announces the outcome.

Other than those professors who serve on the search committee, the rest of the faculty becomes involved at the stage of campus interviews, when heads of departments and sometimes all faculty are invited to meet candidates and pose questions. Here, concerns about teaching should be brought to the fore, although they rarely are mentioned.

To be sure, if candidates were asked whether they were interested in quality of teaching, every one would express concern about the matter. That reply, however, would likely be little more than puffery. What would be crucial are follow-up questions such as these:

1. How should teaching be evaluated?

2. Do you favor a system of peer review?

3. Do you believe graduate departments should offer a practicum for students who wish to be recommended for faculty appointments?

4. How strongly should quality of teaching weigh in the appointment of faculty?

5. Would you ever support giving tenure to a remarkable teacher with a thin publication record?

Only candidates who provide satisfactory answers to such questions should receive the support of the faculty.

I realize, of course, that interviews can be misleading. The candidate who appears confident and genial may turn out in office to be ineffective, evasive, or irresponsible. The rejected candidate whose crusty manner or candid opinions put off some committee members may be offered an administrative position elsewhere and become widely admired for trustworthiness, conscientiousness, and acumen.

Nevertheless, answers to sharp interview questions can be revealing. When a candidate, for example, asserts confidently that student evaluations are crucial but then hems and haws when pushed for comment about peer review, the situation will be clear to all.

The limits of interviews, however, need to be recognized, for the most reliable indicator of future performance is past performance, and the quality of past performance is not found in a brief question-and-answer session that may tell more about the candidate's surface personality and oral facility than sagacity or dependability. In this regard, I recall one administrator I knew who failed at each position held but interviewed brilliantly and was always offered another opportunity, inevitably ending unhappily for the school.

To avoid such egregious errors, search committees should rely most heavily not on impressions garnered from brief conversations but on judgments of individuals who hold posts at the candidate's own campus. What does the chair of the appointments committee say about the candidate's standards for promotions, appointments, and tenure? What do department heads say about how much weight in those decisions the candidate has given to quality of teaching? What do faculty members say about the candidate's attitude toward peer review? During an interview of a few hours, the candidate may maintain a false front to members of a search committee, but those who have long observed the candidate are beyond being fooled.

Thus when the list of finalists is determined, each should be informed that at least one or, better yet, several members of the committee will be speaking to or, preferably, visiting key members of the academic community at the candidate's school. While the individual may request that a particular person not be contacted if thought to be negatively biased, a candidate who objects to the whole procedure should be passed over. For no matter how strong the individual's desire to maintain confidentiality, it is outweighed by the committee's obligation to make the soundest possible decision.

If the information thereby obtained suggests that the administrator's performance at previous institutions displays no interest in enhancing the quality of teaching, the individual is unlikely to care about the matter at the next. To be blunt, when the record is clear, believe it.

In conclusion, imagine a campus where graduate students are taught to fulfill their responsibilities as teachers, where quality of teaching plays an important role in deciding faculty appointments, where teaching skills are evaluated primarily by peer review, where teaching is considered as important as any other criterion in making tenure decisions. and where the administration strongly supports such policies and takes appropriate actions to implement them. There, teaching would not be overshadowed by research but would be illuminated for all to appreciate.

In such circumstances those who paid tuition could depend on receiving the quality of instruction to which they were entitled. What a refreshing change that would be.

# Works by
# Steven M. Cahn

## Books Authored

*Fate, Logic, and Time.*
    Yale University Press, 1967
    Ridgeview Publishing Company, 1982
    Wipf and Stock, 2004
*A New Introduction to Philosophy*
    Harper & Row, 1971
    University Press of America, 1986
    Wipf and Stock Publishers, 2004
*The Eclipse of Excellence: A Critique of American Higher Education*
    (Foreword by Charles Frankel)
    Public Affairs Press, 1973
    Wipf and Stock Publishers, 2004
*Education and the Democratic Ideal*
    Nelson-Hall Company, 1979
    Wipf and Stock, 2004
*Saints and Scamps: Ethics in Academia*
    Rowman & Littlefield, 1986
    Revised edition, 1994
    25th anniversary edition, 2011
    (Foreword by Thomas H. Powell)
*Philosophical Explorations: Freedom, God, and Goodness*
    Prometheus Books, 1989

*Puzzles & Perplexities: Collected Essays*
Rowman & Littlefield, 2002
Second Edition, 2007
*God, Reason, and Religion*
Thomson/Wadsworth, 2006
*From Student to Scholar: A Candid Guide to Becoming a Professor*
(Foreword by Catharine R. Stimpson)
Columbia University Press, 2008
*Polishing Your Prose: How to Turn First Drafts Into Finished Work*
(with Victor L. Cahn)
(Foreword by Mary Ann Caws)
Columbia University Press, 2013
*Happiness and Goodness: Philosophical Reflections on Living Well*
(with Christine Vitrano)
(Foreword by Robert B. Talisse)
Columbia University Press, 2015
*Religion Within Reason*
Columbia University Press, 2017
*Teaching Philosophy: A Guide*
Routledge, 2018
*Inside Academia: Professors, Politics, and Policies*
Rutgers University Press, 2019
*The Road Traveled and Other Essays*
Wipf and Stock Publishers, 2019
*Philosophical Adventures*
Broadview Press, 2019
*A Philosopher's Journey: Essays from Six Decades*
Wipf and Stock Publishers, 2020
*Philosophical Debates*
Wipf and Stock Publishers, 2021
*Navigating Academic Life: How the System Works*
Routledge, 2021
*Professors as Teachers*
Wipf and Stock Publishers, 2022

## Books Edited

*Philosophy of Art and Aesthetics: From Plato to Wittgenstein*
(with Frank A. Tillman)
Harper & Row, 1969
*The Philosophical Foundations of Education*
Harper & Row, 1970
*Philosophy of Religion*
Harper & Row, 1970
*Classics of Western Philosophy*
Hackett Publishing Company, 1977
Second edition, 1985
Third edition, 1990
Fourth edition, 1995
Fifth edition, 1999
Sixth edition, 2003
Seventh edition, 2007
Eighth edition, 2012
*New Studies in the Philosophy of John Dewey*
University Press of New England, 1977
*Scholars Who Teach: The Art of College Teaching*
Nelson-Hall Company, 1978
Wipf and Stock Publishers, 2004
*Contemporary Philosophy of Religion*
(with David Shatz)
Oxford University Press, 1982
*Reason at Work: Introductory Readings in Philosophy*
(with Patricia Kitcher and George Sher)
Harcourt Brace Jovanovich, 1984
Second edition, 1990
Third edition (with Peter J. Markie), 1995
*Morality, Responsibility, and the University: Studies in Academic Ethics*
Temple University Press, 1990
*Affirmative Action and the University: A Philosophical Inquiry*
Temple University Press, 1993

*Twentieth-Century Ethical Theory*
  (with Joram G. Haber)
  Prentice Hall, 1995
*The Affirmative Action Debate*
  Routledge, 1995
  Second edition, 2002
*Classics of Modern Political Theory: Machiavelli to Mill*
  Oxford University Press, 1997
*Classic and Contemporary Readings in the Philosophy of Education*
  McGraw Hill, 1997
  Second edition, Oxford University Press, 2012
*Ethics: History, Theory, and Contemporary Issues*
  (with Peter Markie)
  Oxford University Press, 1998
  Second edition, 2002
  Third edition, 2006
  Fourth edition, 2009
  Fifth edition, 2012
  Sixth edition, 2015
  Seventh edition, 2020
*Exploring Philosophy: An Introductory Anthology*
  Oxford University Press, 2000
  Second edition, 2005
  Third edition, 2009
  Fourth edition, 2012
  Fifth edition, 2015
  Sixth edition, 2018
  Seventh edition, 2021
*Classics of Political and Moral Philosophy*
  Oxford University Press, 2002
  Second edition, 2012
*Questions About God: Today's Philosophers Ponder the Divine*
  (with David Shatz)
  Oxford University Press, 2002

# Works by Steven M. Cahn

*Morality and Public Policy*
(with Tziporah Kasachkoff)
Prentice Hall, 2003
*Knowledge and Reality*
(with Maureen Eckert and Robert Buckley)
Prentice Hall, 2003
*Philosophy for the 21st Century: A Comprehensive Reader*
Oxford University Press, 2003
*Ten Essential Texts in the Philosophy of Religion*
Oxford University Press, 2005
*Political Philosophy: The Essential Texts*
Oxford University Press, 2005
Second edition, 2011
Third edition, 2015
Fourth edition, 2022
*Philosophical Horizons: Introductory Readings*
(with Maureen Eckert)
Thomson/Wadsworth, 2006
Second edition, 2012
*Aesthetics: A Comprehensive Anthology*
(with Aaron Meskin)
Blackwell, 2008
Second edition (with Stephanie Ross and Sandra Shapshay),
2020
*Happiness: Classic and Contemporary Readings*
(with Christine Vitrano)
Oxford University Press, 2008
*The Meaning of Life, 3rd Edition: A Reader*
(with E. M. Klemke)
Oxford University Press, 2008
Fourth edition, 2018
*Seven Masterpieces of Philosophy*
Pearson Longman, 2008
*The Elements of Philosophy: Readings from Past and Present*
(with Tamar Szabó Gendler and Susanna Siegel)
Oxford University Press, 2008

*Exploring Philosophy of Religion: An Introductory Anthology*
   Oxford University Press, 2009
   Second edition, 2016
*Exploring Ethics: An Introductory Anthology*
   Oxford University Press, 2009
   Second edition, 2011
   Third edition, 2014
   Fourth edition, 2017
   Fifth edition, 2020
   Sixth edition, 2023
*Philosophy of Education: The Essential Texts*
   Routledge, 2009
*Political Problems*
   (with Robert B. Talisse)
   Prentice Hall, 2011
*Thinking About Logic: Classic Essays*
   (with Robert B. Talisse and Scott F. Aikin)
   Westview Press, 2011
*Fate, Time, and Language: An Essay on Free Will by David Foster Wallace*
   (with Maureen Eckert)
   Columbia University Press, 2011
*Moral Problems in Higher Education*
   Temple University Press, 2011
   Wipf and Stock Publishers, 2021
*Political Philosophy in the Twenty-First Century*
   (with Robert B. Talisse)
   Westview Press, 2013
*Portraits of American Philosophy*
   Rowman & Littlefield, 2013
*Reason and Religions: Philosophy Looks at the World's Religious Beliefs*
   Wadsworth/Cengage Learning, 2014

*Freedom and the Self: Essays on the Philosophy of David Foster Wallace*
(with Maureen Eckert)
Columbia University Press, 2015
*The World of Philosophy*
Oxford University Press, 2016
Second Edition, 2019
*Principles of Moral Philosophy: Classic and Contemporary Approaches*
(with Andrew T. Forcehimes)
Oxford University Press, 2017
*Foundations of Moral Philosophy: Readings in Metaethics*
(with Andrew T. Forcehimes)
Oxford University Press, 2017
*Exploring Moral Problems: An Introductory Anthology*
(with Andrew T. Forcehimes)
Oxford University Press, 2018
*Philosophers in the Classroom: Essays on Teaching*
(with Alexandra Bradner and Andrew Mills)
Hackett Publishing Company, 2018
*An Annotated Kant: Groundwork for the Metaphysics of Morals*
Rowman & Littlefield, 2020
*The Democracy Reader: From Classical to Contemporary Philosophy*
(with Andrew T. Forcehimes and Robert B. Talisse)
Rowman & Littlefield, 2021
*Academic Ethics Today: Problems, Policies, and Perspectives on University Life*
Rowman & Littlefield, 2022
*Privacy*
(with Carissa Véliz)
Wiley-Blackwell, 2023
*Understanding Kant's* Groundwork
Hackett Publishing Company, 2023

# About the Author

Steven M. Cahn is Professor Emeritus of Philosophy at the City University of New York Graduate Center, where he served for nearly a decade as Provost and Vice President for Academic Affairs, then as Acting President.

He was born in Springfield, Massachusetts, in 1942. His younger years were devoted to music, and he studied piano with Herbert Stessin of the Juilliard School and the noted chamber music artist Artur Balsam. He also became a professional organist under the tutelage of the eminent composer Isadore Freed.

After earning an AB from Columbia College in 1963 and PhD in philosophy from Columbia University in 1966, Dr. Cahn taught at Dartmouth College, Vassar College, New York University, the University of Rochester, and the University of Vermont, where he chaired the Department of Philosophy.

He served as a program officer at the Exxon Education Foundation, as Acting Director for Humanities at the Rockefeller Foundation, and as the first Director of General Programs at the National Endowment for the Humanities. He formerly chaired the American Philosophical Association's Committee on the Teaching of Philosophy, was the Association's delegate to the American Council of Learned Societies, and was longtime President of the John Dewey Foundation, where he initiated the John Dewey Lectures, now delivered at every national meeting of the American Philosophical Association.

Dr. Cahn is the author of twenty books and editor of fifty others. He has also served as general editor of four multivolume series: *Blackwell Philosophy Guides, Blackwell Readings in Philosophy, Issues in Academic Ethics,* and *Critical Essays on the Classics.*

His numerous articles have appeared in a broad spectrum of publications, including *The Journal of Philosophy, The Chronicle of Higher Education, Shakespeare Newsletter, The American Journal of Medicine, The New Republic,* and *The New York Times.*

A collection of essays written in his honor, edited by two of his former doctoral students, Robert B. Talisse of Vanderbilt University and Maureen Eckert of the University of Massachusetts Dartmouth, is titled *A Teacher's Life: Essays for Steven M. Cahn.* His professional autobiography appears in his collection *The Road Traveled and Other Essays.*

# INDEX